drinks

drinks

MURDOCH BOOKS

Contents

Cocktails

Mint julep

Serves 1

ice cubes
60 ml (2 fl oz/¼ cup) bourbon
8 mint leaves
15 ml (½ fl oz) sugar syrup
dash of dark rum or brandy
mint sprig

Half-fill a mixing glass with ice. Add the bourbon, mint and sugar, then stir. Strain into a highball glass filled with ice and stir gently until the glass becomes frosted. Top with a dash of rum or brandy. Garnish with a sprig of mint and serve with a long straw.

Note: Some people like to add a few chunks of cucumber for extra refreshment.

Old fashioned

Serves 1

1 sugar cube
dash of Angostura bitters
soda water
ice cubes
60 ml (2 fl oz/¼ cup) bourbon
orange twist (optional)

Place the sugar cube in an old-fashioned glass. Add the bitters and let it soak into the sugar. Add a splash of soda water and enough ice to half-fill the glass. Pour in the bourbon and stir to dissolve the sugar. Garnish with a twist of orange if you wish.

Corpse reviver

Serves 1

ice cubes
30 ml (1 fl oz) brandy
30 ml (1 fl oz) Calvados
30 ml (1 fl oz) sweet vermouth
apple slices

Half-fill a cocktail shaker with ice. Add the brandy, Calvados and vermouth, shake vigorously and strain into a chilled cocktail glass. Garnish with apple slices.

Stinger

Serves 1

ice cubes or crushed ice
45 ml (1½ fl oz) brandy
15 ml (½ fl oz) white crème de
  menthe
maraschino cherry

Place some ice cubes or crushed ice in a small highball glass. Add the brandy and crème de menthe and stir well. Garnish with a maraschino cherry.

Campari crush

Serves 1

crushed ice
30 ml (1 fl oz) gin
30 ml (1 fl oz) Campari
ruby red grapefruit juice
lime wedge

Fill a highball glass with crushed ice. Add the gin and Campari, then top up with grapefruit juice. Squeeze a lime wedge into the glass and add the squeezed wedge to the drink.

Zoot suit

Serves 1

½ orange, chopped
½ lime, chopped
15 ml (½ fl oz) sugar syrup
ice cubes
45 ml (1½ fl oz) Campari
30 ml (1 fl oz) blood orange juice

Muddle the orange and lime with the sugar syrup in a cocktail shaker. Add a scoop of ice, then the Campari and blood orange juice. Shake vigorously and strain into a chilled tumbler.

Blueberry sour

Serves 1

1 tablespoon lemon sorbet
15 ml (½ fl oz) vodka
chilled Champagne or sparkling wine
6 blueberries

Spoon the sorbet into a chilled martini glass. Pour in the vodka and slowly top up with Champagne or sparkling wine. Garnish with blueberries.

Flirtini

Serves 1

15 ml (½ fl oz) pineapple vodka
15 ml (½ fl oz) pineapple juice
chilled Champagne or sparkling wine
maraschino cherry

Pour the vodka and pineapple juice into a chilled martini glass. Slowly top up with Champagne or sparkling wine and garnish with a maraschino cherry.

Note: Many vodka companies are now producing pineapple vodka, but if you can't find it you can use plain vodka.

Chi chi

Serves 1

crushed ice
45 ml (1 ½ fl oz) vodka
15 ml (½ fl oz) Malibu rum
15 ml (½ fl oz) coconut cream
125 ml (4 fl oz/½ cup) pineapple juice
pineapple wedge
strawberry slices

Place some crushed ice, the vodka, Malibu rum, coconut cream and pineapple juice in a blender and blend well. Pour into a large, chilled tumbler and garnish with a small wedge of pineapple and strawberry slices.

Frankie

Serves 1

ice cubes
15 ml (½ fl oz) Frangelico
15 ml (½ fl oz) Kahlúa
30 ml (1 fl oz) Irish Cream
30 ml (1 fl oz) cream
very finely crushed hazelnuts

Half-fill a cocktail shaker with ice. Add the Frangelico, Kahlúa, Irish Cream and cream. Shake vigorously, then strain into a large chilled cocktail glass. Serve sprinkled with very finely crushed hazelnuts.

Poire royale

Serves 1

15 ml (½ fl oz) Poire William
15 ml (½ fl oz) peach liqueur
1 teaspoon elderflower cordial
chilled Champagne or sparkling wine
thin pear slice

Pour the Poire William, peach liqueur and elderflower cordial into a chilled champagne flute, then slowly top up with Champagne or sparkling wine. Garnish with a pear slice.

Note: You can buy elderflower cordial, or make it at home. Boil 2 litres (70 fl oz/8 cups) water with 1 kg (2 lb 4 oz//4½ cups) sugar until the sugar dissolves and the syrup thickens slightly. Pour it onto six elderflower heads in a sterile glass jar and steep overnight. Strain, add lemon juice to taste and keep refrigerated for a few days. Dilute with water, if necessary.

Raspberry champagne spider

Serves 1

1–2 raspberry sorbet balls
chilled Champagne or sparkling wine

Place one or two balls of raspberry sorbet in a chilled champagne flute and slowly top up with Champagne or sparkling wine.

Note: Scoop a tub of raspberry sorbet into small balls with a melon baller and freeze until needed.

Savoy

Serves 1

15 ml (½ fl oz) Campari
15 ml (½ fl oz) ruby red grapefruit
  juice
15 ml (½ fl oz) lychee juice
chilled Champagne or sparkling wine
orange twist

Pour the Campari, grapefruit juice
and lychee juice into a chilled
champagne flute, then slowly top up
with Champagne or sparkling wine.
Garnish with a twist of orange.

Shampoo

Serves 1

15 ml (½ fl oz) gin
15 ml (½ fl oz) lemon juice
dash of Pernod
dash of blue curaçao
chilled Champagne or sparkling wine
lemon twist

Pour the gin, then the lemon juice, Pernod and blue curaçao into a chilled champagne flute. Slowly top up with Champagne or sparkling wine and garnish with a twist of lemon.

Pineapple, lychee and mint daiquiri

Serves 1

4 mint leaves
45 ml (1½ fl oz) white rum
80 g (3 oz/½ cup) diced fresh
  pineapple
4 lychees, peeled and seeded
15 ml (½ fl oz) pineapple juice
15 ml (½ fl oz) lime juice
15 ml (½ fl oz) sugar syrup
12 ice cubes, crushed
pineapple leaves
mint sprig

Place the mint, rum, pineapple, lychees, pineapple juice, lime juice and sugar syrup in a blender. Add the crushed ice and blend until the mixture is the consistency of shaved ice. Pour into a large chilled cocktail glass and garnish with pineapple leaves and a sprig of mint.

B52

Serves 1

15 ml (½ fl oz) Kahlúa
15 ml (½ fl oz) Irish Cream
15 ml (½ fl oz) Cointreau

Pour the Kahlúa into a shot glass, then carefully float the Irish Cream on top by pouring it over the back of a teaspoon. Using a clean teaspoon, float the Cointreau over the Irish Cream so that you have three distinct layers.

Chocotini

Serves 1

50 g (2 oz) chocolate
ice cubes
60 ml (2 fl oz/¼ cup) vodka
30 ml (1 fl oz) brown crème de cacao

Melt the chocolate in a heatproof bowl over simmering water. Dip the rim of a martini glass in the chocolate, or dot the chocolate around the rim. Chill the glass. Half-fill a cocktail shaker with ice. Add the vodka and crème de cacao, shake vigorously and strain into the chilled martini glass.

Honeycomb

Serves 1

ice cubes
45 ml (1 ½ fl oz) honey vodka
45 ml (1 ½ fl oz) vanilla vodka
15 ml (½ fl oz) sugar syrup
2 vanilla beans

Add a scoop of ice to a cocktail shaker, then the two vodkas and the sugar syrup. Shake vigorously and strain into a chilled martini glass. Garnish with two vanilla beans.

Note: Honey vodka is commercially available but can be hard to obtain. If you can't find it, use extra vanilla vodka, which is more commonly available, or infuse your own.

Japanese slipper

Serves 1

ice cubes
30 ml (1 fl oz) melon liqueur
30 ml (1 fl oz) Cointreau
15 ml (½ fl oz) lemon juice
maraschino cherry

Half-fill a cocktail shaker with ice
Add the melon liqueur, Cointreau and
lemon juice. Shake well and strain into
a chilled cocktail glass. Garnish with a
maraschino cherry.

Malt mafia

Serves 1

2 tablespoons raspberries
10 ml (1/4 fl oz) sugar syrup
ice cubes
45 ml (1 1/2 fl oz) chocolate
  malt vodka
30 ml (1 fl oz) vanilla liqueur
fresh raspberries, to garnish

Muddle the raspberries with the sugar syrup in a cocktail shaker. Add a scoop of ice, then the vodka and vanilla liqueur. Shake vigorously and strain into a chilled tumbler. Garnish with fresh raspberries.

Porto flip

Serves 1

ice cubes
30 ml (1 fl oz) brandy
45 ml (1½ fl oz) red port
egg yolk
freshly grated nutmeg

Half-fill a cocktail shaker with ice.
Add the brandy, port and egg yolk,
then shake vigorously. Strain into
a cocktail glass and sprinkle
with nutmeg.

Rusty nail

Serves 1

ice cubes
45 ml (1½ fl oz) Scotch whisky
45 ml (1½ fl oz) Drambuie
½ orange slice

Half-fill an old-fashioned tumbler with ice. Add the whisky and Drambuie, then garnish with half a slice of orange.

Silk stocking

Serves 1

ice cubes
15 ml (½ fl oz) butterscotch schnapps
15 ml (½ fl oz) advocaat
30 ml (1 fl oz) white crème de cacao
30 ml (1 fl oz) cream
white chocolate shards

Half-fill a cocktail shaker with ice. Add the butterscotch schnapps, advocaat, crème de cacao and cream. Shake vigorously and strain into a chilled martini glass. Garnish with shards of white chocolate.

Full moon

Serves 1

ice cubes
15 ml (½ fl oz) white rum
15 ml (½ fl oz) Kahlúa
1 teaspoon sugar
pinch of ground cloves
pinch of ground cinnamon
150 ml (5 fl oz) cold espresso coffee
15 ml (½ fl oz) cream

Three-quarters fill a highball glass with ice. Add the rum, Kahlúa and sugar and stir well until the sugar has dissolved. Add the cloves and cinnamon, then top up with the coffee. Float the cream over the top by carefully pouring it over the back of a teaspoon.

Mandarini martini

Serves 1

ice cubes
60 ml (2 fl oz/¼ cup) mandarin vodka
10 ml (¼ fl oz) dry vermouth
15 ml (½ fl oz) cranberry juice
orange twist

Half-fill a mixing glass with ice. Add the vodka, dry vermouth and cranberry juice. Stir, strain into a chilled martini glass and garnish with a twist of orange.

Berry Collins

Serves 1

2 tablespoons blueberries
15 ml (½ fl oz) sugar syrup
ice cubes
45 ml (1½ fl oz) gin
30 ml (1 fl oz) vanilla liqueur
15 ml (½ fl oz) lemon juice
cranberry juice or lemonade

Muddle the blueberries with the sugar syrup in a cocktail shaker. Add a scoop of ice, then the gin, vanilla liqueur and lemon juice. Shake vigorously and pour into a tall glass to 2.5 cm (1 inch) from the top, then top up with cranberry juice or lemonade.

Citrus blush

Serves 1

crushed ice
15 ml (½ fl oz) lime juice
15 ml (½ fl oz) limoncello
45 ml (1½ fl oz) gin
ruby red grapefruit juice
lime twist

Half-fill a tall glass with crushed ice. Add the lime juice, limoncello and gin. Stir well to combine, top up with ruby red grapefruit juice and garnish with a twist of lime.

Gimlet

Serves 1

ice cubes
45 ml (1½ fl oz) gin
15 ml (½ fl oz) lime juice
15 ml (½ fl oz) lime juice cordial
lime twist
lime wedge

Half-fill a mixing glass with ice.
Add the gin, lime juice and lime juice
cordial and stir well. Strain into a
chilled goblet and garnish with
a twist of lime and a wedge of lime.

Mint and cucumber martini

Serves 1

8 cucumber slices
10 mint leaves
10 ml (¼ fl oz) sugar syrup
ice cubes
70 ml (2¼ fl oz) gin
10 ml (¼ fl oz) mint-infused dry
  vermouth or plain vermouth
2 cucumber batons

Muddle the cucumber and mint with the sugar syrup in a cocktail shaker. Add a scoop of ice, then the gin. Coat the inside of a chilled martini glass with the vermouth. Place a small sieve over the martini glass and strain the martini into the glass. (This is known as double straining, which ensures a lovely clear drink.) Garnish with two cucumber batons.

Perfect martini

Serves 1

ice cubes
60 ml (2 fl oz/¼ cup) gin
15 ml (½ fl oz) dry vermouth
15 ml (½ fl oz) sweet vermouth
green olives or a lemon twist

Half-fill a mixing glass with ice. Pour in the gin, dry vermouth and sweet vermouth and stir. Strain into a chilled martini glass and garnish with green olives or a twist of lemon.

Red blossom

Serves 1

ice cubes
45 ml (1½ fl oz) gin
15 ml (½ fl oz) peach liqueur
2 tablespoons raspberries
15 ml (½ fl oz) lemon juice
15 ml (½ fl oz) sugar syrup
3 blueberries

Add a scoop of ice to a cocktail shaker, then the gin, peach liqueur, raspberries, lemon juice and sugar syrup. Shake vigorously and strain into a chilled martini glass. Garnish with blueberries.

Singapore Sling

Serves 1

ice cubes
45 ml (1½ fl oz) gin
15 ml (½ fl oz) Bénédictine
15 ml (½ fl oz) Cointreau
15 ml (½ fl oz) cherry brandy
30 ml (1 fl oz) orange juice
30 ml (1 fl oz) pineapple juice
dash of lime juice
dash of grenadine
maraschino cherry

Half-fill a cocktail shaker with ice.
Add all the ingredients except for the
garnish, then shake well and strain
into a tall glass half-filled with ice.
Garnish with a maraschino cherry.

Passionfruit and vanilla vodka jelly shots

Serves 1

1 gelatine leaf
15 ml (½ fl oz) sugar syrup
80 ml (2½ fl oz/⅓ cup) passionfruit
   pulp
80 ml (2½ fl oz/⅓ cup) vanilla vodka

Soak the gelatine leaf in cold water. Heat the sugar syrup and passionfruit pulp until just hot. Squeeze the liquid out of the gelatine, add the gelatine to the passionfruit mixture and stir to dissolve. Cool, stir in the vodka and pour into six shot glasses. Refrigerate for 3 hours, or until set.

Kiwi margarita

Serves 1

egg white
caster (superfine) sugar
crushed ice
45 ml (1½ fl oz) tequila
15 ml (½ fl oz) Cointreau
15 ml (½ fl oz) melon liqueur
15 ml (½ fl oz) lemon juice
1–2 kiwifruit, peeled and chopped
kiwifruit slice

Dip the rim of a cocktail glass in a saucer of egg white, then a saucer of sugar, shaking off any excess. Chill. Place the crushed ice, tequila, Cointreau, melon liqueur, lemon juice and kiwifruit in a blender and blend well. Pour into the sugar-frosted cocktail glass and garnish with a slice of kiwifruit.

Scarlet bellini

Serves 1

15 ml (½ fl oz) peach liqueur
30 ml (1 fl oz) blood orange juice
chilled Champagne or sparkling wine
½ blood orange slice

Pour the peach liqueur and orange juice into a chilled champagne flute. Slowly top up with Champagne or sparkling wine. Garnish with half a slice of blood orange.

Masquerade

Serves 1

ice cubes
45 ml (1½ fl oz) citrus vodka
15 ml (½ fl oz) apple schnapps
30 ml (1 fl oz) watermelon juice
15 ml (½ fl oz) apple juice
dash of lime juice
thin apple slices

Half-fill a cocktail shaker with ice. Add the vodka, apple schnapps, watermelon juice, apple juice and a dash of lime juice. Shake vigorously and strain into a chilled martini glass. Garnish with thin slices of apple.

Sour apple martini

Serves 1

ice cubes
45 ml (1½ fl oz) sweet and sour apple
  schnapps
45 ml (1½ fl oz) vodka
10 ml (¼ fl oz) lime juice
thin apple slice
lime spirals

Half-fill a cocktail shaker with ice.
Add the schnapps, vodka and lime
juice. Shake vigorously and strain into
a chilled martini glass. Garnish with a
floating apple slice and spirals of lime.

Turkish martini

Serves 1

ice cubes
45 ml (1½ fl oz) vanilla vodka
30 ml (1 fl oz) white crème de cacao
10 ml (¼ fl oz) rosewater
small cube of Turkish delight

Add a scoop of ice to a cocktail shaker, then the vodka, crème de cacao and rosewater. Shake vigorously and strain into a chilled martini glass. Garnish with a cube of Turkish delight.

Watermelon and rosewater martini

Serves 1

5 chunks of watermelon
15 ml (½ fl oz) sugar syrup
ice cubes
60 ml (2 fl oz/¼ cup) watermelon-
    infused vodka (see Note)
3 drops of rosewater
3 rose petals

Muddle the watermelon with the
sugar syrup in a cocktail shaker.
Add a scoop of ice, then the vodka
and rosewater. Shake vigorously
and strain into a chilled martini glass.
Garnish with floating rose petals.

Note: To make watermelon-infused
vodka, fill a large, sealable glass jar
with chunks of watermelon flesh and
pour in vodka to cover. Seal and leave
for 5–7 days. Strain and chill.

Cuba libre

Serves 1

ice cubes
60 ml (2 fl oz/¼ cup) white rum
7 lime wedges
cola

Half-fill a highball glass with ice.
Add the rum, squeeze 6 lime wedges
into the glass, then add the squeezed
wedges to the drink. Top up with cola
and garnish with a remaining wedge
of lime.

Acapulco gold

Serves 1

1 lemon, chopped
15 ml (½ fl oz) sugar syrup
ice cubes
45 ml (1½ fl oz) chilli-infused tequila
  (see Note)
15 ml (½ fl oz) vanilla liqueur
lemonade

Muddle the lemon and sugar syrup in a cocktail shaker. Add a scoop of ice, then the tequila and vanilla liqueur. Shake vigorously and strain into a tall, chilled glass 2.5 cm (1 inch) from the top, then top up with lemonade.

Note: To make chilli-infused tequila, place 6 washed and dried fennel fronds and 2 halved small, fresh red chillies in a large sealable glass jar. Fill the jar with tequila and leave for 4–7 days, then strain.

El diablo

Serves 1

ice cubes
60 ml (2 fl oz/¼ cup) tequila
30 ml (1 fl oz) blackcurrant liqueur
ginger ale
lime wedge

Half-fill an old-fashioned glass with ice, add the tequila and blackcurrant liqueur, then top up with ginger ale. Squeeze the lime wedge into the glass, and add the squeezed wedge to the drink. Stir.

Olé

Serves 1

ice cubes
45 ml (1½ fl oz) tequila
30 ml (1 fl oz) banana liqueur
dash of blue curaçao

Half-fill a cocktail shaker with ice.
Add the tequila and banana liqueur,
then shake well. Strain into a small,
chilled cocktail glass. Tip a dash of
blue curaçao into the drink to achieve
a two-tone effect.

Señorita

Serves 1

1 tablespoon raspberries
1 tablespoon blueberries
15 ml (½ fl oz) sugar syrup
ice cubes
45 ml (1½ fl oz) gold tequila
15 ml (½ fl oz) raspberry liqueur
30 ml (1 fl oz) cranberry juice
lime wedge

Muddle berries with the sugar syrup in a cocktail shaker. Add a scoop of ice, then tequila and raspberry liqueur. Shake vigorously and strain into a chilled tumbler 2.5 cm (1 inch) from the top, then top up with cranberry juice. Garnish with a wedge of lime.

Barbados fondue

Serves 1

½ lime, chopped
½ mango, peeled
6 small chunks of young coconut
  flesh
15 ml (½ fl oz) sugar syrup
ice cubes
45 ml (1½ fl oz) peach-infused vodka
30 ml (1 fl oz) guava juice
½ strawberry

Muddle the lime, mango and coconut with the sugar syrup in a cocktail shaker. Add a scoop of ice, then the vodka and guava juice. Shake vigorously, pour into a chilled tumbler and garnish with half a strawberry.

Bloody Mary

Serves 1

3 ice cubes
45 ml (1½ fl oz) vodka
4 drops of Tabasco sauce
1 teaspoon Worcestershire sauce
10 ml (¼ fl oz) lemon juice
pinch of salt
1 grind of black pepper
60 ml (2 fl oz/¼ cup) chilled tomato
  juice
1 crisp celery stalk

Place the ice cubes in a highball glass, pour in the vodka, then add the Tabasco, Worcestershire sauce and lemon juice. Add the salt and pepper, then pour in the tomato juice and stir well. Allow to sit for a minute, then garnish with a stalk of celery.

Note: For extra zing, you could garnish your drink with wedges of lemon and lime.

Caipiroska

Serves 1

1 lime, chopped
3 teaspoons caster (superfine) sugar
15 ml (½ fl oz) sugar syrup
ice cubes
60 ml (2 fl oz/¼ cup) vodka

Muddle the lime with the sugar and sugar syrup in a cocktail shaker. Add a scoop of ice and the vodka. Shake vigorously and strain into a chilled tumbler. Serve with a chunk of lime.

Note: You could make a minty caipiroska by muddling mint leaves with the limes, sugar and sugar syrup.

Diablo

Serves 1

ice cubes
45 ml (1½ fl oz) currant vodka
30 ml (1 fl oz) blackberry liqueur
30 ml (1 fl oz) pineapple juice
pineapple leaf

Add a scoop of ice to a cocktail shaker, then the vodka, blackberry liqueur and pineapple juice. Shake vigorously and strain into a chilled martini glass. Garnish with a pineapple leaf.

Life's good

Serves 1

ice cubes
45 ml (1 1/2 fl oz) sloe berry vodka
15 ml (1/2 fl oz) lychee juice
15 ml (1/2 fl oz) cranberry juice
15 ml (1/2 fl oz) strawberry purée
lime wedge

Half-fill a cocktail shaker with ice.
Add the vodka, lychee juice,
cranberry juice and strawberry purée.
Shake vigorously and strain into a
chilled martini glass. Squeeze the lime
wedge over the drink and add it as
a garnish.

Note: For an after-dinner drink,
sprinkle with grated chocolate —
use dark, milk and white chocolate.

New Yorker

Serves 1

ice cubes
45 ml (1½ fl oz) rye whiskey
1 teaspoon lime juice
dash of grenadine
orange twist

Half-fill a cocktail shaker with ice. Add the rye whiskey, lime juice and grenadine. Shake well, strain into a cocktail glass and garnish with a twist of orange.

Bison kick

Serves 1

ice cubes
45 ml (1 1/2 fl oz) Bison Grass vodka
10 ml (1/4 fl oz) sake
30 ml (1 fl oz) watermelon juice
15 ml (1/2 fl oz) lychee juice
10 ml (1/4 fl oz) sugar syrup
1 peeled fresh lychee

Half-fill a cocktail shaker with ice. Add the vodka, sake, watermelon juice, lychee juice and sugar syrup. Shake vigorously and strain into a chilled cocktail glass. Garnish with a lychee.

Harvey Wallbanger

Serves 1

crushed ice
30 ml (1 fl oz) vodka
10 ml (¹/₄ fl oz) Galliano
orange juice
¹/₂ orange slice

Half-fill a highball glass with crushed ice. Add the vodka and Galliano, then top up with orange juice. Garnish with half a slice of orange.

Mocktails

Blushing peach

Serves 1

125 ml (4 fl oz/½ cup) peach juice
125 ml (4 fl oz/½ cup) almond milk
good dash of Angostura bitters
ice cubes
drizzle of grenadine

Combine the peach juice, almond milk and bitters in a cocktail shaker with 5 large cubes of ice. Shake well, then strain into a medium glass. Drizzle with a little grenadine and use the tip of a knife to gently swirl the grenadine into a pretty pattern.

Cinderella

Serves 1

45 ml (1½ fl oz) orange juice
45 ml (1½ fl oz) pineapple juice
15 ml (½ fl oz) lemon juice
ice cubes

Pour the orange juice, pineapple juice and lemon juice into a cocktail shaker. Add a scoop of ice, shake vigorously, then strain into a chilled martini glass.

Grape bash

Serves 1

10 seedless black grapes
1/2 small lime, chopped
125 ml (4 fl oz/1/2 cup) sparkling
  grape juice

Muddle the grapes and lime in a tall glass until pulpy, then top up with the grape juice.

Lemonade

Serves 1

egg white
caster (superfine) sugar
juice of 1 lemon
juice of 1 lime
soda water
sugar syrup

Dip the rim of two medium glasses in a saucer of egg white, then a saucer of sugar, shaking off any excess. Chill the glasses. Mix the lemon juice and lime juice together in a jug. Pour into the sugar-frosted glasses, then top up with soda water. Stir in sugar syrup to taste.

Mixed berry and pineapple frappé

Serves 1

200 g (7 oz/1½ cups) fresh or frozen
  mixed berries
225 g (8 oz/1⅓ cups) chopped fresh
  pineapple
250 ml (9 fl oz/1 cup) pineapple juice
½ teaspoon rosewater
6–8 ice cubes, crushed

Place berries, pineapple, pineapple juice, rosewater and ice in a blender and blend until smooth. Pour into two tall chilled glasses.

Troppococo

Serves 1

1/2 small mango, peeled and chopped
160 ml (5 fl oz) pink grapefruit juice
60 ml (2 fl oz/1/4 cup) coconut milk
2 teaspoons caster (superfine) sugar
3 large ice cubes

Place the mango, grapefruit juice, coconut milk, sugar and ice in a heavy-duty blender and blend until smooth. Pour into a medium glass.

Juices

Strange bird

Serves 2

500 g (1 lb 2 oz/3½ cups)
  strawberries, hulled
6 kiwifruit, peeled
ice cubes, to serve

Juice the strawberries and kiwifruit through a juice extractor. Stir to combine and serve over ice.

Pine lime and strawberry burst

Serves 2

1 pineapple, peeled
2 limes, peeled
500 g (1 lb 2 oz//3½ cups)
   strawberries, hulled

Juice the pineapple, limes and strawberries through a juice extractor. Stir to combine.

Lemon barley water

Serves 4

110 g (4 oz/½ cup) pearl barley
3 lemons
110 g (4 oz/½ cup) caster sugar
crushed ice, to serve
lemon slices, to garnish

Wash the barley well and place in a medium pan. Using a sharp vegetable peeler, remove the peel from the lemons, avoiding the bitter white pith. Squeeze out the juice and set aside. Add the peel and 1.75 litres (60 fl oz/ 7 cups) cold water to the barley and bring to the boil. Simmer briskly for 30 minutes. Add the sugar and mix well to dissolve. Allow to cool. Strain the liquid into a jug and add the lemon juice. Serve over crushed ice and garnish with lemon slices.

Melon freezie

Serves 4

500 g (1lb 2 oz) rockmelon
500 g (1lb 2 oz) honeydew melon
12 ice cubes
500 ml (17 fl oz/2 cups) orange juice

Remove the rind and seeds from the melons. Cut the flesh into pieces and mix in a blender for 1 minute, or until smooth. Add the ice and orange juice and blend for a further 30 seconds. Transfer to a large shallow plastic dish and freeze for 3 hours. Return the mixture to the blender and blend quickly until smooth. Serve immediately with straws and long spoons.

Mandarin and mango chill

Serves 4

1 mango, cut into slices
500 ml (17 fl oz/2 cups) mandarin
    juice
125 ml (4 fl oz/½ cup) lime juice
    cordial
375 ml (12 fl oz/1½ cups) soda water
2 tablespoons caster sugar
ice cubes, to serve

Freeze the mango for about 1 hour, or
until semi-frozen. Combine the juice,
cordial, soda water and sugar in a jug.
Place the mango slices and some ice
cubes into each glass, then pour in
the juice mix.

Fennel and orange juice

Serves 2

8 oranges
150 g (5 oz) baby fennel

Peel and quarter the oranges, and remove any seeds. Trim the fennel and cut in half. Using a juicer, push the fennel through first to release the flavours, then juice the orange. Chill well. Mix together well before serving.

Note: When fennel is in season, the flavour will be stronger in larger, more developed fennel.

Pear, apple and ginger juice

Serves 2

3 cm (1 inch) piece ginger
3 ripe pears, cored, quartered, chilled
5 Granny Smith apples, quartered,
   chilled

Using a juicer, juice the ginger, pear and apple pieces together. Pour into a jug. Mix together well and then serve immediately.

Pineapple kick

Serves 2

3 oranges, peeled
600 g (1lb 5 oz/4 cups) chopped
   fresh pineapple
3.5 cm (1½ inch) piece ginger

Cut the oranges into pieces to fit the
juicer. Using the plunger, push the
orange pieces, pineapple and ginger
through the juicer and into a jug.
Pour into glasses and serve with ice.

Virgin Mary

Serves 4

750 ml (26 fl oz/3 cups) tomato juice
1 tablespoon Worcestershire sauce
2 tablespoons lemon juice
1/4 teaspoon ground nutmeg
few drops Tabasco sauce
12 ice cubes
2 lemon slices, halved

Place tomato juice, Worcestershire sauce, lemon juice, nutmeg and the Tabasco sauce in a large jug and stir until combined. Place the ice cubes in a blender and blend for 30 seconds, or until the ice is crushed down to half a cup. Pour the tomato juice mixture into serving glasses and add the crushed ice and lemon slices. Season with salt and pepper before serving.

Morning blended fruit juice

Serves 4

½ pineapple, peeled and cored
375 ml (13 fl oz/1½ cups) orange
  juice
1 large pear, chopped
1 banana, chopped
40 g (1½ oz) chopped pawpaw

Chop the pineapple flesh into pieces
and place in the blender. Add the
orange juice, pear, banana and
pawpaw and blend until smooth.
Serve immediately.

Honeydew melon and passionfruit

Serves 4

750 g (1lb 10 oz) honeydew melon
  (about 1 whole medium fruit)
6 passionfruit (see Note)
ice cubes, to serve

Peel and seed the melon. Cut into pieces to fit the juicer. Halve the passionfruit and scoop out the pulp. Feed melon pieces through juicer and stir through the passionfruit pulp. Chill well. Serve in a jug with lots of ice.

Note: The amount of passionfruit pulp depends on the fruit. If passionfruit are not juicy use one 120 g (4 oz) can passionfruit pulp.

Green apple and lemon thirst quencher

Serves 2

80 ml (3 fl oz/$\frac{1}{3}$ cup) lemon juice, chilled
6 green apples chilled
mint leaves, to garnish

Pour the lemon juice into the serving jug. Wash the apples and cut into smaller pieces to fit into the juicer. Using the plunger, push the apples through the juicer. Add the apple juice to lemon juice and stir well. Garnish with mint leaves. Serve immediately.

Note: This is a refreshing, slightly tart drink. If the apples and lemons are not cold, throw a handful of ice cubes into the blender and pulse.

Blackcurrant crush

Serves 4

750 ml (26 fl oz/3 cups) apple and
  blackcurrant juice
500 ml (17 fl oz/2 cups) soda water
1 tablespoon caster sugar
150 g (5 oz) blueberries
ice cubes, to serve

Place the apple and blackcurrant
juice, soda water, sugar and
blueberries into a blender and blend
until smooth. Serve in chilled glasses
over ice.

Mint julep

Serves 4

1 large handful fresh mint leaves
1 tablespoon sugar
1 tablespoon lemon juice
250 ml (9 fl oz/1 cup) pineapple juice
250 ml (9 fl oz/1 cup) ginger ale
ice cubes, to serve
mint leaves, to garnish

Roughly chop mint leaves and place them in a heatproof jug along with the sugar. Using a wooden spoon, bruise the mint. Add 125 ml (4 fl oz/½ cup) boiling water, the pineapple juice and the lemon juice. Mix well. Cover with plastic wrap and leave for 30 minutes. Strain, then refrigerate until cold.

Just before serving, add the ginger ale and mix well. Serve in glasses over ice and garnish with mint leaves.

Green punch

Serves 2

1 green apple, cored
1/2 honeydew melon, peeled, seeds
  removed
2 oranges, peeled
ice cubes, to serve

Cut the apple, melon and oranges into pieces to fit the juicer. Using the plunger, push all ingredients through the juicer and into a jug. Pour into glasses and serve with ice.

Too good for you

Serves 2

1 large apple, cored
6 carrots, tops removed
4 celery sticks, including leaves
6 iceberg lettuce leaves
20 English spinach leaves

Cut apple, carrots and celery sticks to fit the juicer. Using the plunger, push all the ingredients through the juicer and into a large jug. Pour into glasses and serve with ice, if desired.

Celery, tomato and parsley juice

Serves 2

1 large handful fresh parsley
6 vine-ripened tomatoes, quartered
4 celery sticks, trimmed

Using a juicer, push through the parsley leaves to infuse the flavour. Then juice the tomatoes and celery. Chill well. Before serving, mix together well and garnish with a stick of celery as a swizzle stick.

Note: For extra spice, add a few drops of Tabasco and freshly ground black pepper.

Pineapple and coconut iced drink

Serves 2

500 ml (17 fl oz/2 cups) pineapple
  juice
250 ml (9 fl oz/1 cup) coconut milk
mint leaves, to garnish
pineapple leaves, to garnish

Combine the pineapple juice with the coconut milk in a large jug and mix well. Pour 125 ml (4 fl oz/$\frac{1}{2}$ cup) of the mixture into 8 holes of an ice cube tray and freeze. Chill the remaining mixture in refrigerator. When the ice cubes have frozen, pour the chilled juice mixture into 2 glasses, add the frozen cubes and garnish with mint and pineapple leaves.

Blue moon

Serves 2

300 g (11 oz) blueberries
6 small peaches, stones removed
2 cm (³/₄ inch) piece ginger
pinch ground cinnamon
honey, to taste, optional
ice cubes, to serve

Juice the blueberries, peaches and ginger through a juice extractor. Stir through the cinnamon and honey, if desired, and serve over ice.

Cherry blossom slushy

Serves 2

3 large nashi pears, stalks removed
300 g (11 oz) frozen pitted cherries
8–10 ice cubes, crushed

Juice the nashi through a juice extractor. Add the nashi juice, frozen cherries and ice cubes to a blender and process until smooth.

Red grape and rockmelon juice

Serves 2

500 g (1 lb 2 oz) red seedless grapes
1 rockmelon (or other orange-fleshed
   melon), peeled, seeded and chopped
2 cm (^{3}/$_4$ inch) piece ginger

Juice the grapes, rockmelon and
ginger through a juice extractor.
Stir to combine.

R'n'r

Serves 2

300 g (11 oz) frozen raspberries
juice of 1 lime
½ rockmelon (or other orange-fleshed
   melon), peeled, seeded and
   chopped
1 teaspoon honey

Blend the frozen raspberries with the lime juice in a blender in short bursts until the berries are starting to break up. Add a little water, if necessary, to help blend the berries. Add rockmelon and honey and blend until smooth.

Minted apple orchard

Serves 2

6 apples, stalks removed
3 pears, stalks removed
1 large handful mint leaves, plus extra
  to garnish

Juice the apples, pears and mint leaves through a juice extractor. Stir to combine and drink straight away. Garnish with a sprig of mint, if desired.

Apricot fruit spritzer

Serves 4

500 ml (17 fl oz/2 cups) apricot nectar
250 ml (9 fl oz/1 cup) apple juice
250 ml (9 fl oz/1 cup) orange juice
500 ml (17 fl oz/2 cups) soda water
8 ice cubes

Put apricot nectar, apple juice, orange juice, soda water and ice cubes into a large jug and stir to combine.

Perfumed nectarine

Serves 2

6 large nectarines, stones removed
4 peaches, stones removed
250 g (9 oz) lychees, peeled
  and seeded

Juice the nectarines, peaches and
lychees through a juice extractor.
Save one thin slice of nectarine for
garnishing, if desired. Stir to combine.

Pear, melon and peppermint juice

Serves 2

3 pears, stalks removed
½ small rockmelon (or other
    orange-fleshed melon), peeled,
    seeded and chopped
few peppermint leaves
ice cubes, to serve

Juice the pears, rockmelon and peppermint leaves through a juice extractor. Stir to combine and serve over ice.

Note: The best way to select a ripe melon is to use your nose. If it has a strong, sweet fragrance and thick raised netting you can almost guarantee it is ready to eat.

Sweet and spicy plum

Serves 2

10 small plums, stones removed
3 cm (1¼ inch) piece ginger
200 g (7 oz) cherries, pitted
3 oranges, peeled
1 large handful mint leaves
1 teaspoon honey
ice cubes, to serve

Juice the plums, ginger, cherries, oranges and mint through a juice extractor. Stir through the honey, mixing well, and serve over ice.

Banana, kiwi and lemon frappé

Serves 2

2 bananas, chopped
3 kiwifruit, peeled and chopped
4 scoops lemon sorbet

Blend the banana, kiwifruit and sorbet in a blender until smooth.

Honeydew, pineapple and mint juice

Serves 4

1 honeydew melon, peeled, seeded
  and chopped
1 small pineapple, peeled
1 handful mint leaves

Juice the honeydew, pineapple and
mint leaves through a juice extractor.
Stir to combine.

Mango summer haze

Serves 4

2 mangoes, chopped
500 ml (17 fl oz/2 cups) orange juice
55 g (2 oz/¼ cup) caster (superfine)
  sugar
500 ml (17 fl oz/2 cups) sparkling
  mineral water
ice cubes, to serve
mango slices, to garnish, optional

Blend mango, orange juice and sugar in a blender until smooth. Stir through the mineral water. Serve over ice and garnish with mango slices, if desired.

Passionfruit syrup

Serves 4

6 panama or large passionfruit
125 ml (4 fl oz/½ cup) lemon juice
115 g (4 oz/½ cup) caster (superfine)
  sugar

Combine the passionfruit pulp, lemon juice, sugar and 500 ml (17 fl oz/2 cups) water in a saucepan over high heat. Stir until all the sugar has dissolved. Bring to the boil, reduce to a simmer and then cook for 1½ hours or until reduced by half and slightly syrupy. Allow to cool, then strain, pressing on the solids. Pour into a sterilised glass jar or bottle and seal. Refrigerate for up to 2 weeks.

Note: To serve, pour a little syrup into a glass with ice and top with soda water, lemonade or dry ginger ale.

Fresh pineapple juice with mandarin sorbet

Serves 2

1 large pineapple, peeled
250 ml (9 fl oz/1 cup) dry ginger ale
4 scoops mandarin sorbet

Juice the pineapple through a juice extractor. Combine the pineapple juice and dry ginger ale in a large jug and chill. Stir to combine, pour into 2 glasses and top each with 2 scoops of sorbet.

Watermelon and strawberry slushy

Serves 6

2 kg (4 lb 8 oz) chopped watermelon (about 1 large watermelon)
250 g (9 oz/1²/₃ cups) strawberries, hulled
2 teaspoons caster (superfine) sugar

Combine watermelon, strawberries and sugar in a bowl. Save some of the watermelon for garnishing. Blend the mixture in batches in a blender until smooth, then pour into a shallow metal tray. Cover with plastic wrap and freeze for 2–3 hours, or until the mixture begins to freeze. Return to blender and blend quickly to break up the ice. Pour into 6 glasses, then cut the reserved watermelon into 6 small triangles and fix one onto the edge of each glass.

Think pink

Serves 2

3 pink grapefruit, peeled
250 g (9 oz/1²/₃) strawberries, hulled
375 ml (13 fl oz/1½ cups) guava juice
ice cubes, to serve

Juice the grapefruit and strawberries through a juice extractor. Stir through the guava juice and serve over ice.

Orange citrus crush

Serves 4

12 navel oranges (see Note)
zest and juice of 1 lime
sugar, to taste
ice cubes, to serve

Segment 2 of the oranges and juice the remainder in a citrus press — don't strain the juice, you can keep the pulp in it. Add the lime zest and juice to the orange juice. Add the orange segments and sugar. Stir to combine and serve over ice.

Note: The juice of navel oranges will turn bitter within minutes of juicing, so drink this juice immediately. Use blood oranges when they're in season.

Orange sorbet soda

Serves 2

500 ml (17 fl oz/2 cups) orange juice
250 ml (9 fl oz/1 cup) lemonade
2–4 scoops lemon sorbet

Combine the orange juice and
lemonade in a jug. Pour into
2 large glasses and top each with
1–2 scoops of sorbet.

Mandarin and passionfruit shots

Serves 4

6 mandarins, peeled
1 panama or large passionfruit

Juice the mandarins through a juice extractor. Strain the passionfruit pulp and discard the seeds, reserving a few for garnish if desired. Stir the passionfruit juice through the mandarin juice and chill well. Stir to combine and serve in a shot glass garnished with the reserved passionfruit seeds, if desired.

Vitalising beetroot, carrot and ginger juice

Serves 2

1 beetroot, scrubbed
6 carrots
3 cm (1¼ inch) piece ginger, peeled

Juice the beetroot, carrots and ginger through a juice extractor. Stir to combine.

Honeyed carrots

Serves 2

1 kg (2 lb 4 oz) carrots
125 g (5 oz) alfalfa sprouts
4 pears, stalks removed
1–2 teaspoons honey, to taste

Juice the carrots, alfalfa and pears through a juice extractor. Stir through the honey. Garnish with carrot strips, if desired.

Green machine

Serves 2

6 celery stalks
2 apples, stalks removed
125 g (5 oz) alfalfa sprouts
1 handful flat-leaf (Italian) parsley
1 handful mint leaves

Juice the celery, apples, alfalfa, parsley and mint through a juice extractor. Stir to combine.

Cool as a cucumber

Serves 2

3 large cucumbers
3 limes, peeled
1 large handful mint leaves
1 1/2 tablespoons caster
  (superfine) sugar

Juice the cucumbers, limes and mint through a juice extractor. Stir through the sugar.

Fuzzy peach

Serves 2

6 peaches, stones removed
1 lemon, peeled
large pinch freshly grated nutmeg
250 ml (9 fl oz/1 cup) dry ginger ale
ice cubes, to serve

Juice the peaches and lemon through
a juice extractor. Stir through the
nutmeg and the dry ginger ale. Serve
over ice.

Kiwi delight

Serves 4

3 kiwifruit, peeled and sliced
80 g (3 oz/½ cup) chopped pineapple
1 banana, chopped
250 ml (9 fl oz/1 cup) tropical fruit
   juice
2 ice cubes

Blend the kiwifruit, pineapple, banana, fruit juice and ice cubes in a blender until smooth.

Green shot

Serves 6

1 very large handful flat-leaf (Italian)
  parsley
1 cucumber
½ teaspoon caster (superfine) sugar
½ teaspoon lemon juice

Juice the parsley and cucumber
through a juice extractor, saving a
little cucumber for garnishing. Stir
through the sugar until the sugar
has fully dissolved. Chill well, then
stir through the lemon juice and
garnish with cucumber sticks.
Serve immediately in shot glasses.

Basil, spearmint and liquorice wake-me-up

Serves 2

1 tablespoon liquorice tea leaves
1 tablespoon spearmint tea leaves
10 basil leaves
basil leaves, extra, to serve

Put the liquorice and spearmint tea leaves into a teapot. Lightly crush the basil leaves and add them to the pot. Fill the pot with boiling water (about 1 litre/35 fl oz/4 cups), put on the lid and leave to brew for 3 minutes. Strain into teacups and garnish with basil leaves. Serve hot or cold.

Note: As the tea cools, the liquorice flavour becomes stronger and sweeter — add a few slices of lemon if you find it too strong.

Spinach energiser

Serves 2

50 g (2 oz/1 cup) baby English
  spinach leaves
1 large cucumber
3 apples, stalks removed
3 celery stalks
1 baby fennel
1 handful parsley

Juice the spinach, cucumber, apples,
celery, fennel and parsley through a
juice extractor. Stir to combine.

Gazpacho in a glass

Serves 2

6 vine-ripened tomatoes
1 red capsicum (pepper)
1 lemon, peeled
2 large cucumbers
1 handful parsley
1 garlic clove
dash Tabasco sauce
ice cubes, to serve
extra virgin olive oil, to serve, optional

Juice tomatoes, capsicum, lemon, cucumbers, parsley and garlic through a juice extractor. Stir through the Tabasco, to taste. Serve over ice with a drizzle of extra virgin olive oil, if desired.

Cinnamon, maple and pear frappé

Serves 2

400 g (14 oz) canned pears in
  natural juice
1/2 teaspoon ground cinnamon
1 1/2 tablespoons pure maple syrup
12 large ice cubes

Blend the pears and juice, maple
syrup, cinnamon and ice cubes in
a blender until smooth.

Red ginger

Serves 4

500 g (1 lb 2 oz) red seedless grapes
10 small plums, stones removed
2 limes, peeled
3 cm (1¼ inch) piece ginger
1 handful mint leaves
ice cubes, to serve

Juice the grapes, plums, limes, ginger and mint through a juice extractor. Stir to combine and serve over ice in shot glasses.

Warm ginger and carrot shots

Serves 8 (shot glasses)
  or 2 (large glasses)

2 kg (4 lb 8 oz) carrots
4 cm (1½ inch) piece ginger
1 tablespoon lemon juice
large pinch ground cinnamon
large pinch ground cumin
natural yoghurt, to serve, optional

Juice carrots and ginger through a juice extractor. Transfer to a saucepan with the lemon juice, cinnamon and cumin. Stir over medium heat until just warmed through then pour into shot glasses or tall glasses. Top each glass with a small dollop of yoghurt and slightly swirl through.

Vanilla and apricot orange infusion

Serves 6

200 g (7 oz) dried apricots, chopped
1 vanilla bean, chopped
zest of 1 orange
55 g (2 oz/¼ cup) caster (superfine) sugar
small pinch cloves, optional
ice cubes, to serve

Combine the apricots, vanilla bean, orange zest, sugar, cloves and 3 litres (105 fl oz/12 cups) water in a large saucepan. Stir over high heat until the sugar has dissolved. Bring to the boil, then reduce the heat and gently simmer for 20 minutes. Set aside to cool. Strain and chill well. Stir to combine and serve over ice.

Hawaiian crush

Serves 2

100 g (4 oz) papaya, peeled, seeded
  and chopped
200 g (7 oz/1 cup) chopped
  watermelon
250 ml (9 fl oz/1 cup) apple juice
6 large ice cubes

Blend the papaya, watermelon, apple
juice and ice cubes in a blender until
smooth. Chill well.

Lemon soother

Serves 4

½ lemon, thinly sliced
1 large lemon thyme sprig
1 stem lemongrass, bruised
honey, to taste, optional

Put the lemon, lemon thyme and lemongrass in the base of a large heatproof jug and pour in 1 litre (35 fl oz/4 cups) boiling water. Set aside to infuse for 10–15 minutes. Serve hot or warm with some honey, if desired.

Watermelon breakfast juice

Serves 2

700 g (1 lb 9 oz/3½ cups) chopped
  watermelon
2 tablespoons lime juice
1–2 cm (½–¾ inch) piece ginger,
  grated, to taste
2 tablespoons chopped mint

Blend the watermelon, lime juice,
ginger and mint in a blender in short
bursts. (Be careful not to overblend
or the mixture will go frothy.)

Smoothies

Blue maple

Serves 2

200 g (7 oz/1 cup) low-fat blueberry
  fromage frais
185 ml (6 fl oz/³/₄ cup) low-fat milk
1 tablespoon maple syrup
½ teaspoon ground cinnamon
300 g (11 oz) frozen blueberries

Blend the fromage frais, milk, maple
syrup, cinnamon and 250 g (9 oz) of
the frozen blueberries in a blender
until smooth. Serve topped with the
remaining blueberries.

Apple and cinnamon shake

Serves 2

250 ml (9 fl oz/1 cup) apple juice
2 tablespoons natural yoghurt
185 ml (6 fl oz/³⁄₄ cup) milk
3 scoops vanilla ice cream
pinch of cinnamon

Blend the apple juice, yoghurt, milk and ice cream in a blender until they are well combined and fluffy. Top with a sprinkle of cinnamon.

Good start to the day

Serves 4

2 bananas, chopped
1 large mango, chopped
500 ml (17 fl oz/2 cups) skim milk
500 ml (17 fl oz/2 cups) orange juice
  or pink grapefruit juice

Blend the banana, mango, milk and orange or pink grapefruit juice in a blender until smooth. Pour into a jug and chill.

Watermelon smoothie

Serves 4

600 g (1 lb 5 oz/3 cups) chopped
  watermelon
125 g (5 oz/½ cup) yoghurt
250 ml (9 fl oz/1 cup) milk
1 tablespoon caster (superfine) sugar
2 scoops vanilla ice cream

Blend the watermelon, yoghurt, milk
and sugar in a blender until smooth.
Add the ice cream and blend for a few
seconds, or until frothy.

Note: Use seedless watermelon, if
possible. Otherwise, pick out as many
seeds as you can before blending.

Passionfruit ice cream soda

Serves 2

6 passionfruit
625 ml (22 fl oz/2½ cups) lemonade
2–4 scoops vanilla ice cream

Combine 125 ml (4 fl oz/½ cup) passionfruit pulp with the lemonade, pour into 2 glasses and top each with 1–2 scoops of ice cream. Serve with straws and long spoons.

Cranberry, raspberry and vanilla slushy

Serves 2

500 ml (17 fl oz/2 cups) cranberry
  juice
300 g (11 oz) frozen raspberries
1 tablespoon caster (superfine) sugar
200 g (7 oz) vanilla yoghurt
about 10 ice cubes, crushed

Blend the cranberry juice, frozen raspberries, sugar, yoghurt and ice cubes in a blender until smooth.

Note: To make your own vanilla yoghurt, simply scrape the seeds from a vanilla bean into a large tub of natural yoghurt, add the pod and refrigerate overnight.

Summer strawberry smoothie

Serves 2

250 g (9 oz/1¹⁄₃ cups) strawberries,
   hulled
250 ml (9 fl oz/1 cup) wildberry
   drinking yoghurt
4 scoops strawberry frozen yoghurt
1 tablespoon strawberry sauce
few drops natural vanilla extract
   (essence)
ice cubes, to serve

Blend the strawberries, yoghurt,
frozen yoghurt, strawberry flavouring
and vanilla in a blender until thick and
smooth. Serve over ice.

Peachy egg nog

Serves 4

2 eggs, separated
60 ml (2 fl oz/¼ cup) milk
55 g (2 oz/¼ cup) caster (superfine)
  sugar
80 ml (3 fl oz/⅓ cup) cream
440 ml (16 fl oz/1¾ cups) peach
  nectar
2 tablespoons orange juice
ground nutmeg, to garnish

Beat egg yolks, milk and half the sugar in a bowl. Put the bowl over a pan of simmering water — do not allow base of the bowl to touch the water. Cook, stirring, for 8 minutes, or until the custard thickens. Remove from the heat, cover the surface with plastic wrap and set aside to cool.

Beat the egg whites until frothy. Add remaining sugar, to taste, then beat until stiff peaks form. In a separate bowl, whip the cream until soft peaks form. Gently fold the egg whites and cream into the cooled custard. Stir through peach nectar and the orange juice. Cover and chill for 2 hours. Beat the mixture lightly. Serve sprinkled with nutmeg.

Creamy rich banana and macadamia smoothie

Serves 2

2 very ripe bananas, slightly frozen
100 g (4 oz) honey-roasted
  macadamias
2 tablespoons vanilla honey yoghurt
500 ml (17 fl oz/2 cups) milk
2 tablespoons wheat germ
1 banana, extra, halved lengthways

Blend the frozen bananas, 60 g (2 oz) of the macadamias, yoghurt, milk and wheat germ in a blender for several minutes until thick and creamy. Finely chop remaining macadamias and put on a plate. Toss the banana halves in the nuts to coat. Stand a banana half in each glass or stand on the glass edge. Pour in the smoothie.

Note: The bananas need to be very ripe. Peel and chop them, toss in lemon juice and freeze in an airtight container ready for use later on.

Avocado smoothie

Serves 2

1 small avocado, peeled, stone
   removed
500 ml (17 fl oz/2 cups) milk
3 teaspoons honey
½ teaspoon natural vanilla extract
   (essence)

Blend the avocado, milk, honey and
vanilla in a blender until smooth.

Apricot crumble smoothie

Serves 2

200 g (7 oz) canned apricots in
  natural juice
200 g (7 oz) vanilla yoghurt
250 ml (9 fl oz/1 cup) milk
1 tablespoon wheat germ
1 tablespoon malted milk powder
large pinch ground cinnamon

Blend the undrained apricots,
yoghurt, milk, wheat germ, malted
milk powder and cinnamon in a
blender until smooth.

Note: Canned peaches, apples
or pears can be used instead
of apricots.

Coconut cream and raspberry shake

Serves 4

300 g (11 oz) raspberries
250 ml (9 fl oz/1 cup) apple and
  blackcurrant juice
400 ml (14 fl oz) coconut cream
2 scoops vanilla soy ice cream
marshmallows, to serve

Blend the raspberries, apple and blackcurrant juice, coconut cream and ice cream in a blender for several minutes until thick and creamy. Thread marshmallows onto 4 swizzle sticks and serve with the shakes, along with a straw and a long spoon.

Note: For a low-fat drink, blend the raspberries and juice with ice instead of coconut cream and ice cream.

Almond cherry smoothie

Serves 2

375 ml (13 fl oz/1½ cups) almond
  milk
400 g (14 oz) cherries, pitted
¼ teaspoon natural vanilla
  extract (essence)
pinch ground cinnamon
4 large ice cubes

Blend the almond milk, cherries,
vanilla, cinnamon and ice cubes
in a blender until smooth.

Note: If you like a strong almond
or marzipan flavour, add a dash
of almond extract (essence).

Banana soy latte

Serves 4

440 ml (16 fl oz/1¾ cups) coffee-
flavoured soy milk
2 bananas, chopped
8 large ice cubes
1 teaspoon drinking chocolate
¼ teaspoon ground cinnamon

Blend the soy milk and banana in a blender until smooth. With the blender running, add the ice cubes one at a time until well incorporated. Serve sprinkled with the drinking chocolate and ground cinnamon.

Carob peanut smoothie

Serves 2

400 ml (14 fl oz) carob – or
    chocolate – flavoured soy milk
2 very ripe bananas, chopped
150 g (5 oz) silken tofu
2 tablespoons honey
1 tablespoon peanut butter

Blend the soy milk, banana, tofu,
honey and peanut butter in a blender
until smooth.

Pineapple and lychee creamy colada

Serves 6

1/3 pineapple, peeled and chopped
750 ml (26 fl oz/3 cups) pineapple
 juice
500 g (1 lb 2 oz) canned lychees
2 tablespoons spearmint leaves
125 ml (4 fl oz/1/2 cup) coconut cream
crushed ice

Blend the pineapple, pineapple juice, lychees and their juice and spearmint in a blender until smooth. Add the coconut cream and crushed ice and blend until thick and smooth.

Strawberry lassi

Serves 2

250 g (9 oz/1²/₃ cups) strawberries,
  hulled
300 g (11 oz) strawberry soy yoghurt
2 tablespoons honey
4 ice cubes

Blend strawberries, yoghurt, honey,
ice cubes and 2½ tablespoons water
in a blender until smooth. Garnish
with any remaining strawberries.

Passionfruit and vanilla ice cream whip

Serves 2

4 passionfruit
100 g (4 oz) passionfruit yoghurt
500 ml (17 fl oz/2 cups) milk
1 tablespoon caster sugar
2 scoops vanilla ice cream

Scoop out the pulp from the passionfruit and push through a sieve to remove seeds. Place into blender with the yoghurt, milk, sugar and ice cream and blend until smooth. Pour into tall glasses and serve with an extra scoop of ice cream, if desired.

Cranberry and vanilla ice cream spider

Serves 4

500 ml (17 fl oz/2 cups) cranberry
  juice
500 ml (17 fl oz/2 cups) soda water
4 scoops vanilla ice cream
185 ml (6 fl oz/³/₄ cup) cream
1 tablespoon caster sugar
20 g (1 oz) flaked almonds, toasted

Combine the juice and soda water in a jug. Add a scoop of ice cream to each tall glass. Pour the juice and soda over the ice cream. Whip the cream and sugar until soft peaks form. Spoon over the juice and soda and top with a sprinkle of almonds.

Melon shake

Serves 2

500 g (1 lb 2 oz) rockmelon, peeled
  and seeded
2 tablespoons honey
375 ml (13 fl oz/1½ cups) milk
5 scoops vanilla ice cream
ground nutmeg, to garnish

Cut the rockmelon into 2 cm (1 inch) pieces and place in a blender. Mix for 30 seconds, or until smooth. Add the honey, milk and ice cream and blend for a further 10–20 seconds, or until well combined and smooth. Serve sprinkled with nutmeg.

Summer buttermilk smoothie

Serves 2

350 g (12 oz) rockmelon
2 peaches, peeled and sliced
150 g (5 oz/1 cup) strawberries,
  roughly chopped
4 mint leaves
125 ml (4 fl oz/½ cup) buttermilk
125 ml (4 fl oz/½ cup) orange juice
1–2 tablespoons honey

Remove the rind and the seeds from the rockmelon and cut the flesh into pieces. Place rockmelon, peaches, strawberries and the mint leaves in a blender and blend until smooth. Add the buttermilk, the orange juice and 1 tablespoon of the honey and blend to combine. Taste for sweetness and add more honey, if needed.

Apricot whip

Serves 3

75 g (2½ oz) dried apricots
125 g (5 oz/½ cup) apricot yoghurt
170 ml (6 fl oz/⅔ cup) light coconut
  milk
310 ml (11 fl oz/1¼ cups) milk
1 tablespoon honey
1 scoop vanilla ice cream
flaked coconut, toasted, to garnish

Cover the apricots with boiling water and soak for 15 minutes. Drain and then roughly chop. Place the apricots, yoghurt, coconut milk, milk, honey and ice cream in a blender and blend until smooth. Pour into tall, chilled glasses and sprinkle with the flaked coconut, as desired.

Mango smoothie with fresh berries

Serves 4

2 mangoes, peeled and seeded
125 ml (4 fl oz/½ cup) milk
250 ml (9 fl oz/1 cup) buttermilk
1 tablespoon caster sugar
2 scoops mango gelati or sorbet
50 g (2 oz/⅓ cup) blueberries

Place the mango, milk, buttermilk, sugar and the gelati in a blender and then blend until smooth. Pour into chilled glasses and serve garnished with the blueberries.

Banana date smoothie

Serves 2

250 g (9 oz/1 cup) low-fat plain
  yoghurt
125 ml (4 fl oz/½ cup) skim milk
50 g (2 oz/½ cup) fresh dates, pitted
  and chopped
2 bananas, sliced
8 ice cubes

Place the yoghurt, milk, dates,
banana and ice cubes in a blender.
Blend until the mixture is smooth
and the ice cubes have been well
incorporated. Serve in chilled glasses.

Wild berries

Serves 4

250 g (9 oz/1 cup) low-fat strawberry
  yoghurt
125 ml (4 fl oz/½ cup) cranberry juice,
  chilled
250 g (9 oz/1⅔ cups) strawberries,
  hulled and quartered
125 g (5 oz) frozen raspberries

Combine the yoghurt and cranberry
juice in a blender. Add strawberries
and 80 g (3 oz) of the raspberries.
Blend until smooth. Pour into chilled
glasses and top with the remaining
frozen raspberries. Serve with a
spoon as it is quite thick.

Plum and prune tang

Serves 4

250 g (9 fl oz/1 cup) low-fat vanilla
  yoghurt
125 ml (4 fl oz/½ cup) buttermilk
310 ml (11 fl oz/1¼ cups) milk
150 g (5 oz/1 cup) prunes, pitted and
  diced
200 g (7 oz/½ cup) diced fresh plums
8 large ice cubes

Place the yoghurt, buttermilk, milk,
prunes, plums and ice cubes in a
blender. Blend until the mixture is
smooth and the ice cubes have been
well incorporated. Serve immediately.

Big bold banana

Serves 4

750 ml (26 fl oz/3 cups) soy milk,
  chilled
125 g (5 oz) soft silken tofu
4 very ripe bananas, sliced
1 tablespoon honey
1 tablespoon vanilla essence
1 tablespoon carob powder
  (see Note)

Combine the soy milk and tofu in
a blender. Add the banana, honey,
vanilla essence and carob powdor.
Blend until smooth. Serve in tall
chilled glasses with a long spoon.

Note: Carob powder is available from
health food stores.

Island shake

Serves 2

400 g (14 oz) fresh mango pulp
125 ml (4 fl oz/½ cup) fresh lime juice
125 ml (4 fl oz/½ cup) coconut milk
2 teaspoons honey
3 teaspoons finely chopped fresh mint
200 g (7 oz) ice cubes

Place the mango pulp, lime juice, coconut milk, honey, mint and ice in a blender and blend until smooth. Chill well and serve.

Iced honey coffee

Serves 2

375 ml (13 fl oz/1½ cups) very strong
  (double strength) fresh coffee
2 tablespoons honey
375 ml (13 fl oz/1½ cups) milk
caster sugar, to taste

Pour the hot coffee into a heatproof
jug and add the honey. Stir until the
honey has totally dissolved, then chill
in the refrigerator. Add the milk and
taste for sweetness. Add a little caster
sugar if necessary. Pour about 125 ml
(4 fl oz/½ cup) of the mixture into
8 holes of an ice cube tray and freeze.
Meanwhile, chill the remaining mixture
in the refrigerator. When ready to serve,
place four coffee ice cubes in each
glass, then pour in the iced coffee.

Smoothberry

Serves 4

150 g (5 oz/1 cup) strawberries,
  hulled
60 g (2 oz/½ cup) raspberries
200 g (7 oz) boysenberries
250 ml (9 fl oz/1 cup) milk
3 scoops vanilla ice cream

Place the strawberries, raspberries, boysenberries, milk and ice cream in a blender and blend until smooth. Chill. Pour into glasses and serve.

Note: If boysenberries are unavailable, any other berry can be used.

Iced chocolate

Serves 1

2 tablespoons rich chocolate topping
375 ml (13 fl oz/1½ cups) icy-cold
  milk
1 scoop vanilla ice cream
whipped cream, to serve
drinking chocolate, to serve

Pour the chocolate topping into a glass
and swirl it around the sides. Fill with
the cold milk and add the ice cream.
Serve with a big swirl of whipped
cream and dust with drinking chocolate.

Papaya and orange smoothie

Serves 2

1 papaya (650 g/1 lb 7 oz)
1 orange
6–8 ice cubes
200 g (7 oz) plain yoghurt
1–2 tablespoons caster sugar
ground nutmeg, to garnish

Peel the papaya and remove the seeds. Cut the flesh into cubes. Peel the orange and roughly chop the flesh. Place the papaya, orange and ice in a blender and blend until smooth. Blend in the yoghurt, and add sugar, to taste. Divide between two glasses, sprinkle lightly with nutmeg and serve.

Note: This keeps well for 6 hours in the fridge and is best in both flavour and colour when small Fijian papaya are used. Peach or apricot flavoured yoghurt may be used for added flavour.

Sports shake

Serves 2

500 ml (17 fl oz/2 cups) milk, chilled
2 tablespoons honey
2 eggs
½ teaspoon natural vanilla essence
  (extract)
1 tablespoon wheat germ
1 banana, sliced

Blend the milk, honey, eggs, vanilla,
wheat germ and banana until smooth.
Chill well and serve.

Peanut choc power

Serves 4

500 ml (17 fl oz/2 cups) chocolate-
flavoured soy milk, chilled
125 g (5 oz) soft silken tofu
60 g (2 oz/¼ cup) smooth peanut
butter
2 bananas, sliced
2 tablespoons chocolate syrup
8 large ice cubes

Combine the soy milk, tofu and
peanut butter in a blender. Add the
banana, chocolate syrup and ice
cubes. Blend until smooth.

Blueberry starter

Serves 2

200 g (7 oz) fresh or frozen
  blueberries
250 g (9 oz/1 cup) plain yoghurt
250 ml (9 fl oz/1 cup) milk
1 tablespoon wheat germ
1–2 teaspoons honey, or to taste

Blend berries, yoghurt, milk, wheat germ and honey until smooth. Pour into glasses and serve immediately.

Note: Frozen blueberries are great for this recipe. There is no need to thaw, just throw into the blender frozen.

Strawberry shake

Serves 2

1 tablespoon strawberry flavouring
170 ml (6 fl oz/^{2}/$_3$ cup) cold milk
80 ml (3 fl oz/^{1}/$_3$ cup) cream
2 scoops strawberry ice cream

Blend strawberry flavouring, milk, cream and 2 scoops strawberry ice cream in a blender until smooth. Serve in chilled glasses.

Breakfast shake

Serves 2

150 g (5 oz) fruit (passionfruit, mango,
  banana, peaches, strawberries,
  blueberries)
250 ml (9 fl oz/1 cup) milk
2 teaspoons wheat germ
1 tablespoon honey
60 g (2 oz/¼ cup) vanilla yoghurt
1 egg, optional
1 tablespoon malt powder

Blend all the ingredients in a blender
for 30–60 seconds, or until well
combined. Pour into chilled glasses
and serve immediately.

Honeycomb smoothie

Serves 2

310 ml (11 fl oz/1¼ cups) cold milk
125 g (5 oz/½ cup) plain Greek-style
  yoghurt
2 teaspoons honey
70 g (3 oz) chocolate honeycomb bar,
  roughly chopped
3 scoops vanilla ice cream

Blend all the ingredients in a blender
until smooth. Serve immediately.

Apple and blackcurrant shake

Serves 2

250 ml (9 fl oz/1 cup) apple and
   blackcurrant juice
185 ml (6 fl oz/³/₄ cup) milk
2 tablespoons plain yoghurt
3 scoops vanilla ice cream

Blend the apple and blackcurrant
juice, milk, yoghurt and ice cream in a
blender until well combined and fluffy.
Serve immediately.

Cinnamon and custard shake

Serves 2

375 ml (13 fl oz/1 1/2 cups) milk
185 ml (6 fl oz/3/4 cup) prepared
  custard
3 teaspoons honey
1 1/2 teaspoons ground cinnamon
3 scoops vanilla ice cream
ground cinnamon, extra, to serve

Blend the milk, custard, honey, cinnamon and ice cream until smooth and fluffy. Pour into tall glasses, sprinkle with extra cinnamon and serve immediately.

Choc cherry smoothie

Serves 2

500 ml (17 fl oz/2 cups) milk
55 g (2 oz/¼ cup) red glacé cherries
25 g (1 oz/¼ cup) desiccated
  coconut
1 tablespoon chocolate topping
3 scoops chocolate ice cream

Blend the milk, cherries, coconut, topping and ice cream until smooth and fluffy. Pour into tall glasses and serve immediately.

Choc caramel smoothie

Serves 2

375 ml (13 fl oz/1½ cups) cold milk
100 g (4 oz) chocolate-covered
  caramel nougat bar, roughly
  chopped
2 teaspoons chocolate topping
4 scoops chocolate ice cream

Blend the milk, chocolate bar,
chocolate topping and ice cream until
smooth. Serve immediately.

Note: There will still be some small
pieces of chocolate after blending.

Coconut and passionfruit smoothie

Serves 2

140 ml (5 fl oz) coconut milk
250 ml (9 fl oz/1 cup) milk
25 g (1 oz/¼ cup) desiccated
  coconut
¼ teaspoon natural vanilla essence
  (extract)
3 scoops vanilla ice cream
170 g (6 oz) can passionfruit pulp
  in syrup

Blend the coconut milk, the milk, the coconut, the vanilla, the ice cream and half the passionfruit pulp until smooth and fluffy. Stir in the remaining pulp and serve immediately.

Apricot tofu smoothie

Serves 2

4 apricots, halved and stoned
2 peaches, halved and stoned
250 ml (9 fl oz/1 cup) apricot nectar,
  chilled
150 g (5 oz) silken tofu

Place the apricots, peaches, nectar
and tofu in a blender and blend until
smooth. Pour into glasses and serve.

Decadent swirled chocolate thickshake

Serves 4

250 ml (9 fl oz/1 cup) milk
1 1/4 tablespoons chocolate syrup
5 scoops chocolate ice cream
35 g (1 oz) chocolate-coated peppermint crisp bar, roughly chopped
1 tablespoon chopped fresh mint
5 scoops vanilla ice cream

Blend half the milk with the chocolate syrup and chocolate ice cream. Pour into 4 glasses. Blend the peppermint crisp bar with the remaining milk, mint and vanilla ice cream. Pour over the chocolate mixture and swirl together to combine. Serve immediately with a straw.

Coconut and lime lassi

Serves 2

400 ml (14 fl oz) coconut milk
185 g (7 oz/3/4 cup) plain yoghurt
60 ml (2 fl oz/1/4 cup) fresh lime juice
60 g (2 fl oz/1/4 cup) caster sugar
8–10 ice cubes
lime slices, to garnish

Blend the coconut milk, yoghurt, lime juice, sugar and ice cubes until the mixture is well combined and the ice cubes are well crushed. Pour into tall glasses and serve immediately, garnished with slices of fresh lime.

Island blend

Serves 2

100 g (4 oz) chopped fresh pineapple
½ small papaya, seeded and
  chopped
2 small bananas, sliced
60 ml (2 fl oz/¼ cup) coconut milk
250 ml (9 fl oz/1 cup) orange juice
ice cubes, to serve

Cut the pineapple and papaya into
smaller chunks and place in a blender.
Add the banana and coconut milk and
blend until smooth. Add orange juice
and blend until combined. Pour into
glasses and serve with ice.

Chocoholic thickshake

Serves 2

125 ml (4 fl oz/½ cup) cold milk
50 g (2 oz) dark chocolate, grated
2 tablespoons chocolate syrup
2 tablespoons cream
4 scoops chocolate ice cream
2 scoops chocolate ice cream, extra
grated dark chocolate, extra, to serve

Blend the milk, chocolate, syrup, cream and ice cream in a blender until smooth. Pour into chilled glasses. Top each glass with a scoop of ice cream and sprinkle with grated chocolate.

Lemonades

Lavender and rose lemonade

Serves 6

juice and zest of 2 lemons
15 g (½ oz) English lavender flowers,
  stripped from their stems
110 g (4 oz/1½ cups) sugar
½ teaspoon rosewater
edible pale pink rose petals,
  to garnish, optional

Put the lemon zest, lavender flowers, sugar and 500 ml (17 fl oz/2 cups) boiling water into a heatproof jug and mix well. Cover with plastic wrap and set aside for 15 minutes. Strain, then stir through lemon juice, rosewater and enough cold water to make 1 litre (35 fl oz/4 cups). Chill well. Stir to combine and serve garnished with rose petals, if desired.

Note: Add more water, if preferred, for a milder flavour.

Homemade lemonade

Serves 6

685 ml (24 fl oz/2¾ cups) lemon juice
275 g (10 oz/1¼ cups) caster
  (superfine) sugar
ice cubes, to serve
mint leaves, to garnish

Combine the lemon juice and sugar in a large bowl and stir until the sugar has dissolved. Pour into a large jug. Add 1.25 litres (44 fl oz/5 cups) water, stir well and chill. Serve over ice, garnished with a few mint leaves.

Mixed berry and lemonade fizz

Serves 4

50 g (2 oz/^{1}/$_3$ cup) fresh blueberries
100 g (4 oz/^{2}/$_3$ cup) strawberries,
  hulled
750 ml (26 fl oz/3 cups) lemonade
2 scoops lemon sorbet

Place the berries, lemonade and lemon sorbet into a blender and purée until well combined. Pour into cold glasses and serve immediately with extra berries, if desired.

Raspberry lemonade

Serves 6

300 g (11 oz) fresh or frozen
   raspberries, thawed
275 g (10 oz/1¼ cups) sugar
500 ml (17 fl oz/2 cups) lemon juice
ice cubes, to serve
mint leaves, to garnish

Combine raspberries and sugar in a blender and blend until smooth. Place a strong sieve over a large bowl and push the mixture through to remove seeds. Discard seeds.Add the lemon juice and mix well. Pour into a large jug and stir in 1.5 litres (52 fl oz/ 6 cups) water, then refrigerate until cold. To serve, pour over ice cubes and garnish with mint leaves.

Coffees

Espresso

This is a single shot of concentrated dark-coloured coffee, topped with a light brown foamy crema, formed by the pressure with which the water is forced through the coffee. The crema should be resilient enough to hold a spoonful of sugar for a couple of seconds.

Variations: Americano is diluted with hot water, also known as caffee grande or a long espresso. Ristretto is an extra long espresso. Romano is served with a twist of lemon peel. Coretto is espresso 'corrected' with a dash of amaretto, sambucca or grappa.

Spiced coffee with a kick

Serves 2

2 sugar cubes
40 ml (1 1/2 fl oz) rum
125 ml (4 fl oz/1/2 cup) espresso or
    strong filtered coffee, hot
pinch of ground cloves
pinch of ground cinnamon
pinch of ground ginger
1/2 teaspoon vanilla sugar
grated orange rind, optional
whipped cream, optional

Put the sugar cubes into a cup and add rum. Add the spices and pour the hot espresso or coffee into cup. Mix until sugar has dissolved. Add the grated orange rind, if desired. Top with whipped cream.

Caffe latte freddo

Hot espresso is mixed with cold milk
– the proportions are one-third
espresso to two-thirds milk – and
shaken with ice. Ideally, the coffee
should be strained into a large glass,
but you can serve it with ice, if you
prefer. Serve with a couple of
long straws.

Caffe freddo

A shot of espresso (sweetened if
desired, while hot), which is cooled
down by shaking with ice in a cocktail
shaker. The coffee is then quickly
strained into a chilled glass – the
coffee will have a fine layer of crema.
Caffe freddo is served at the end of
an evening meal.

Espresso macchiato

A shot of espresso, served in a small glass or cup 'stained' (which is what macchiato means) with a dab of hot milk froth. Despite being officially a milky coffee, one can just about get away with drinking this after dinner, even in Italy where such things are frowned upon!

Coffee granita

This is a grainy iced coffee. Mix 300 ml (11 fl oz) of freshly made espresso with 200 g (7 oz/1 cup) soft brown sugar and 50 ml (2 fl oz) brandy, then freeze, stirring every two hours until a light crystal texture is formed. Serve with a spoon as a delicious, cool end to a meal.

Froth it up

Once upon a time you needed a coffee machine with a steaming device to froth the milk for a cappuccino or latte – even then the pressure was never quite strong enough! Perversely, in the high-tech 21st century, we have found an easier way: a cafetière can froth up milk brilliantly. Skimmed milk works best. Warm it in a pan to just below boiling point and transfer it to a cafetière so that the milk comes one-third of the way up — you must leave room for the milk to expand. Pump the plunger about 10 times to create your froth. Leftover milk cannot be reheated and refrothed. Small battery-operated hand held milk frothers can also be used – these are really good – but for the ultimate low-tech solution, just pour the heated milk into a plastic mineral water bottle, close tight and shake away.

Cappuccino

This is about one-third espresso, one-third hot milk topped with one-third froth. This should not be extremely milky and the flavour of the coffee should come through. A true aficionado would never sprinkle the foam with chocolate, as is often seen in coffee shops.

Note: When milk is added to an espresso, the coffee takes on a whole new meaning – a new drink is created and the flavour of the coffee is given a different tone. The addition of milk can even affect the time of day that the coffee is consumed. Most milky coffees are considered breakfast fare, to the extent that drinking a cappuccino after midday in Italy is a real no-no.

Caffe latte

One part espresso to four parts milk –
milkier-tasting than the cappuccino.
The milk and coffee should be poured
simultaneously into a thick glass. This
drink has largely been popularised by
the many American-style coffee shops
that have appeared in recent years.

Café au lait

This is a popular breakfast drink in
France as well as in Spain, where it's
known as cafe con leche. Made by
topping a shot of espresso with hot
milk, it is usually served in a bowl.
This is nearly every European child's
introduction to the world of coffee.

Teas

Iced orange and strawberry tea

Serves 4

3 oranges, peeled
500 g (1 lb 2 oz/1²/₃ cups)
  strawberries, hulled
2 orange pekoe tea bags
ice cubes, to serve
orange zest, to garnish, optional

Juice the oranges and strawberries through a juice extractor. Put the tea bags and 1.25 litres (44 fl oz/5 cups) boiling water in a heatproof bowl. Set aside to infuse for 5 minutes. Discard the tea bags. Stir through the orange and strawberry juice. Chill well. Stir to combine and serve over ice with a twist of orange zest, if desired.

Iced kiwi green tea

Serves 4

6 kiwifruit, peeled
1 lemon, thinly sliced
2 green tea bags
2 tablespoons caster (superfine) sugar
ice cubes, to serve
kiwifruit slices, to serve
lemon slices, to serve

Juice the kiwifruit through a juice extractor. Put the lemon slices, tea bags and 1.25 litres (44 fl oz/5 cups) boiling water into a heatproof bowl. Set aside to infuse for 5 minutes. Strain and discard the tea bags. Add the kiwifruit juice and sugar and stir until the sugar has dissolved. Set aside to cool, then chill. Stir to combine and serve over ice, garnished with a slice each of kiwifruit and lemon.

Orange and cardamom herbal tea

Serves 2

3 cardamom pods
250 ml (9 fl oz/1 cup) orange juice
3 strips orange rind
2 tablespoons caster (superfine) sugar

Place the cardamom pods on a chopping board and press with the side of a large knife to crack them open. Place the cardamom, orange juice, rind, sugar and 500 ml (17 fl oz/2 cups) water in a pan and stir over medium heat for 10 minutes, or until the sugar has dissolved. Bring to the boil then remove from the heat. Leave to infuse for 2–3 hours, or until cold. Chill in the refrigerator. Strain and serve over ice.

Apple and cinnamon herbal tea

Serves 2

4 (600 g/1 lb 5 oz) golden delicious
  apples, roughly chopped
1 cinnamon stick
3–4 tablespoons soft brown sugar
ice cubes, to serve

Place apple, cinnamon stick, sugar
and 1 litre (35 fl oz/4 cups) water in a
pan. Bring to the boil, then reduce the
heat and simmer for 10–15 minutes,
or until the flavours have infused and
the apples have softened. Remove
from the heat, cool slightly, then chill
in the refrigerator until cold. When
cold, strain and serve over lots of ice.

Orange and ginger tea cooler

Serves 2

1 small orange
½–1 tablespoon Darjeeling tea leaves
250 ml (9 fl oz/1 cup) ginger beer
8 thin slices glacé ginger
2 tablespoons sugar
4–6 ice cubes
mint leaves, to garnish

Remove peel from the orange using a vegetable peeler, avoiding the white pith, and cut into long thin strips. Place half the peel and tea leaves in a bowl and pour in 500 ml (17 fl oz/ 2 cups) boiling water. Cover and leave to steep for 5 minutes, then strain through a fine strainer. Pour into a jug, add ginger beer and chill for 6 hours, or preferably overnight. One hour before serving, add the ginger, the sugar and the remaining orange peel. Stir well. Pour into tall glasses, add 2–3 ice cubes per glass and garnish with mint leaves.

Moroccan mint tea

Serves 1

1 tablespoon green tea leaves
30 g (1 oz) sugar
1 large handful of spearmint leaves
and stalks

Heat the teapot and add the green tea leaves, sugar and spearmint leaves and stalks. Fill with boiling water and brew for at least 5 minutes. Adjust the sweetness if necessary.

Note: In Morocco, this light sweet tea is often served before, and always after every meal, and is prepared at any hour of the day when friends or guests arrive at a Moroccan home. It is sipped in cafés. Traditionally it is served from a silver teapot into ornately painted glasses.

Lemongrass tea

Serves 2

3 lemongrass stalks
2 slices lemon
3 teaspoons honey, or to taste
lemon slices, extra, to serve

Prepare the lemongrass by removing the first two tough outer layers. For maximum flavour, only use the bottom one-third of the stalk (the white part). Slice the lemongrass thinly into rings. (The remaining stalks can be used as a garnish, if desired.)

Place the lemongrass in a jug and cover with 625 ml (22 fl oz/2½ cups) boiling water. Add the lemon slices and cover. Allow to infuse and cool. When cooled to room temperature, strain. Add the honey, to taste. Place the tea in the refrigerator to chill.

To serve, pour the tea into two glasses with extra slices of lemon. Add ice, if desired.

Iced mint tea

Serves 6

4 peppermint tea bags
80 ml (3 fl oz/⅓ cup) honey
500 ml (17 fl oz/2 cups) grapefruit
  juice
250 ml (9 fl oz/1 cup) orange juice
mint sprigs, to garnish

Place the tea bags in a large heatproof jug and pour in 750 ml (25 fl oz/3 cups) boiling water. Allow to steep for 3 minutes, then remove and discard the bags. Stir in the honey and allow to cool. Add the grapefruit and orange juice. Cover and chill in the refrigerator. Serve in glasses, garnished with fresh mint.

American iced tea

Serves 8

4 Ceylon tea bags
2 tablespoons sugar
2 tablespoons lemon juice
375 ml (13 fl oz/1½ cups) dark grape
  juice
500 ml (17 fl oz/2 cups) orange juice
375 ml (13 fl oz/1½ cups) ginger ale
lemon slices, to serve

Place the tea bags in a heatproof
bowl with 1 litre (35 fl oz/4 cups)
boiling water. Leave for 3 minutes.
Remove the bags and stir in sugar.
Cool. Stir in juices. Refrigerate until
cold, then add the ginger ale. Serve
over ice cubes with a slice of lemon.

Earl Grey summer tea

Serves 4

1 cinnamon stick
1 tablespoon Earl Grey tea leaves
250 ml (9 fl oz/1 cup) orange juice
2 teaspoons finely grated orange rind
2 tablespoons sugar, to taste
ice cubes, to serve
1 orange, sliced into thin rounds
4 cinnamon sticks, extra, to garnish

Place the cinnamon stick, tea leaves, orange juice, orange rind and 750 ml (26 fl oz/3 cups) water in a medium pan. Slowly bring to a simmer over gentle heat. Once simmering, stir in the sugar, to taste, and stir until dissolved. Remove from the heat and allow to cool. Once the mixture has cooled, strain the liquid into a jug and refrigerate until cold.

Serve in a jug with lots of ice cubes, garnished with the orange slices and extra cinnamon stick.

Iced lemon and peppermint tea

Serves 2

2 peppermint tea bags
6 strips lemon rind (2 x 5 cm/
    1 x 2 inches)
1 tablespoon sugar, to taste
ice cubes, to serve
mint leaves, to garnish

Place the tea bags and lemon rind strips in a large bowl. Covor with 830 ml (29 oz/3⅓ cups) boiling water and leave to infuse for 5 minutes. Squeeze out the tea bags and discard. Stir in the sugar to taste. Pour into a jug and chill. Serve in chilled glasses with ice cubes and mint leaves.

Punch
& Mulled Wine

Pimm's punch

Serves 10

375 ml (13 fl oz/1 ½ cups) orange
  juice
ice cubes
400 ml (14 fl oz) Pimm's No. 1
400 ml (14 fl oz) bourbon
185 ml (6 fl oz/¾ cup) sweet
  vermouth
185 ml (6 fl oz/¾ cup) white rum
1 bottle of Champagne or sparkling
  wine
500 g (1 lb 2 oz/3 cups) chopped
  fresh fruit and vegetables (such
  as a combination of kiwifruit,
  strawberries, lemon and cucumber)

Freeze 90 ml (3 oz) of the orange juice
in an ice-cube tray. Half-fill a punch
bowl with ice, then add the Pimm's,
bourbon, vermouth, rum, remaining
orange juice and the Champagne or
sparkling wine. Stir in the fresh fruit
and vegetables and the frozen orange
juice ice cubes.

Mulled wine

Serves 6

12 cloves
2 oranges
60 g (2 oz/¼ cup) sugar
1 whole nutmeg, grated
4 cinnamon sticks
2 lemons, thinly sliced
750 ml (26 fl oz/3 cups) full-bodied
   red wine

Push the cloves into the oranges and place in a saucepan with the sugar, nutmeg, cinnamon sticks and lemon. Pour in 500 ml (17 fl oz/2 cups) water and bring to the boil, then reduce the heat, cover the pan and simmer for 20 minutes. Allow to cool, then strain and discard the fruit and spices. Pour the mixture into a saucepan, add the full-bodied red wine and heat until almost boiling — do not allow to boil or the alcohol will evaporate. Serve in heatproof glasses.

Buttered rum

Serves 4

1 tablespoon sugar
250 ml (9 fl oz/1 cup) rum
1–2 teaspoons softened unsalted
  butter

Place the sugar, rum and 500 ml
(17 fl oz/2 cups) boiling water in
a heatproof jug. Stir to dissolve
the sugar, then divide among four
mugs. Stir the butter into each mug
and serve.

Berry and cherry punch

Serves 10

1 lemon
425 g (15 oz) tinned pitted black
  cherries
125 g (5 oz) halved strawberries
600 g (1 lb 5 oz) assorted fresh or
  frozen berries
500 ml (17 fl oz/2 cups) lemonade
750 ml (26 fl oz/3 cups) ginger ale
250 ml (9 fl oz/1 cup) cold black tea
10 torn mint leaves
ice cubes, to serve

Peel the skin from the lemon with a
vegetable peeler, avoiding the bitter
white pith. Cut into long thin strips.
Drain the black cherries and put in
a large bowl. Add the strawberries,
berries, lemonade, ginger ale, tea,
mint leaves and the lemon zest.
Cover and chill for at least 3 hours.
Add ice cubes when serving.

Index

INDEX

INDEX

INDEX

Published in 2010 by Murdoch Books Pty Limited

Murdoch Books Australia
Pier 8/9, 23 Hickson Road
Millers Point NSW 2000
Phone: +61 (0)2 8220 2000
Fax: +61 (0)2 8220 2558
www.murdochbooks.com.au

Murdoch Books UK Limited
Erico House, 6th Floor
93–99 Upper Richmond Road
Putney, London SW15 2TG
Phone: +44 (0)20 8785 5995
Fax: +44 (0)20 8785 5985
www.murdochbooks.co.uk

Chief Executive: Juliet Rogers

Publisher: Lynn Lewis
Senior Designer: Heather Menzies
Photography (cover): Stuart Scott
Stylist (cover): Louise Bickle
Editor: Justine Harding
Editorial Coordinator: Liz Malcolm
Production: Kita George

National Library of Australia Cataloguing-in-Publication Data
Title: Drinks. ISBN: 978-1-74196-950-4 (pbk.)
Series: Chunky series. Subjects: Beverages. Dewey Number: 641.87

Printed by 1010 Printing International.
PRINTED IN CHINA

Cover credits: Vintage fabrics, Major & Tom.
Yellow bowl, Mud Australia

IMPORTANT: Those who might be at risk from the effects of salmonella poisoning (the elderly, pregnant
women, young children and those suffering from immune deficiency diseases) should consult their doctor
with any concerns about eating raw eggs.

OVEN GUIDE: You may find cooking times vary depending on the oven you are using. For fan-forced
ovens, as a general rule, set the oven temperature to 20°C (35°F) lower than indicated in the recipe.